100
KEYS TO
GREAT
FABRIC
PAINTING

JULIA RICHARDSON

NORTH LIGHT BOOKS
Cincinnati, Ohio

Contents

INTRODUCTION

FABRICS HAVE BEEN decorated and embellished since the earliest times when primitive people used extracts from leaves, twigs, berries and roots to color the material they wove into clothes and blankets. Over a thousand years ago, the Javanese developed a technique, known as batik, to make colorful printed fabrics, and similar "resist dye" processes were known to the ancient Egyptians and early Chinese. Many of today's techniques have their roots in ancient times, when brilliant results were achieved without sophisticated tools and machinery. These simple fabric decorating methods are as effective today as they ever were.

In the 1960s color burst on the scene, and a whole new generation adopted the ancient technique of tie-dyeing and made it their own. No two patterns were the same. The appeal of tie-dyeing lay in its simplicity and the amazing results that could be achieved by even the most inexperienced person. That's what this book is about. It is full of simple ideas to help both the beginner and the more experienced crafter to achieve fantastic results.

Tie-dyeing is perhaps the most satisfying of all the fabric decorating techniques. Virtually anything you have in the house can be used as a canvas on which to create vivid explosions of color – an old T-shirt you may be about to throw away or a large piece of fabric that can be turned into a fantastic throw. This book will guide you through the basic rules of fabric dyeing and introduce you to some of the short-cuts and time-saving tips that I've picked up over the years.

If you're already an accomplished artist, fabric painting can offer you a whole new canvas. The ideas in the fabric painting section are for experienced artists, who can always use a few fresh hints on new techniques, as well as for the novice who wants to know where to start. It provides an overview of the different kinds of products on the market, together with hints on how to get the best out of them.

As you become more confident, you can move on to fabric printing and batik. Craft stores are widespread all over the place, and the tools I describe are freely available.

The best part of fabric decorating is experimenting. I hope that the tips I've given will make that experimenting all the more fun and creative. The book is designed to be easy to use. Wherever possible, pictures show the techniques and what the results look like. But don't be deterred if your design doesn't look exactly the same. That's the beauty of fabric decoration – every piece is different. So dive in, try it, and don't be afraid to improvise. Whether you tie-dye a small cotton handkerchief or produce a large batik bedspread, enjoy yourself! The real pleasure of fabric decorating is that not only do you get to look at your results, you get to wear them, sleep in them, sit on them and eat off them as well. Have fun!

TIE-DYEING

This is one of the oldest known methods of decorating fabric. Although the most basic tie-dye techniques evoke memories of the Sixties and hippy rock festivals, there are many tie-dye techniques that give very sophisticated results. Tie-dye is a "resist" method of dyeing, and its success relies on keeping the dye away from selected areas of the fabric so that the resisted area provides the design. It is one of the easiest yet most dynamic ways of creating both simple and intricate patterns.

1 **CHOOSING DYES** Different dyes are made for different fabric types. Delicate fabrics, silk for instance, require hand dyeing, unlike cotton which can be dyed in the washing machine with a machine dye, while synthetic fabrics always have to be dyed by hand. For the best results, remember to check the fabric content before you buy the dye, and always read the instructions on the package.

2 **DYE MIXING** There is no need to hunt for fresh colors when you want a particular shade. Dyes from the same line can be mixed to create new colors. Treat the powder as you would any other medium in terms of the rules of color mixing (i.e., red and blue make purple). Varying the ratios of the colors will produce shades of the intermediate color. Achieving a specific shade will take some practice before you can be certain of the result.

3 **TRUE COLORS** If the colors of your tie-dyed garments are not as bright and vivid as you expected, this may be because of the material. Pure, natural fabrics will give the most vibrant true-to-package-color results, while mixed-fiber fabrics will produce lighter shades.

4 **AMOUNT OF DYE** The quantity of dye you need is dictated by the weight of the fabric, so it is vital to weigh your fabric before you go to the store so you can figure out how many packs of dye you will need. Guidance will always be available in the package instructions.

100% cotton.   **Polyester-cotton blend.**

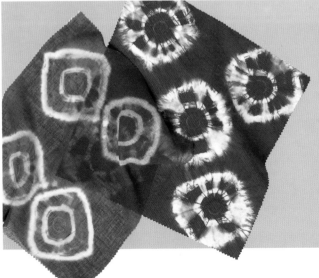

5 **FABRIC WEAVE** The nature of a fabric has a strong bearing on its tie-die pattern. Loosely woven fabrics such as gauze will give softer patterns when tied than fabrics with a heavier weave such as denim. Stretch fabrics distort when wet so they give less predictable results.

6 **REMOVING COLOR** If your fabric is not color-fast, you can start from scratch by removing the original color with a color stripper. Always read the label on the package for full usage instructions.

Color stripping.

7 **COLOR CORRECTION** If you are disappointed by the finished color of your dyed fabrics and find that they are not the same as the color on the dye pack, this is probably because of the original color of the fabric. The general rules of dyeing follow the standard rules of color mixing, a yellow fabric dyed blue will turn out green and a red fabric dyed blue will end up purple.

8 **SETTING THE DYE** Some dyes, mostly cold water ones, have to be set. Make sure you buy the right quantity of fixative – again, instructions on the dye pack will guide you. As a general rule, any dyes applied to fabrics in any way other than by immersion as described on the package instructions will produce a less colorfast result. So be sure to wash your dyed garments separately.

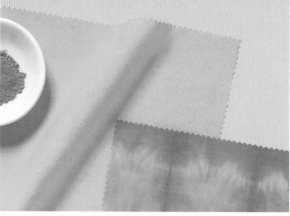

9 **FABRIC PREPARATION** Before you start, always wash your fabric to remove any finishes and preparations added during its manufacture. Iron the fabric before you tie it so that you are working from a clean and smooth "canvas," though for larger pieces of fabric that will be machine dyed this is not strictly necessary. Creases in the fabric before you begin to tie will affect the final result. It also helps to start the tying process with your fabric fully dampened to prevent patches.

10 **COVERING UP** Dyes are made from very fine powder which has an immediate coloring effect that is hard to remove from your hands and clothes, so always put on rubber gloves and an apron before you open the package.

11 **LOOSE AND TIGHT TIES** All bindings and ties are based on the principle of binding tightly to resist or keep the dye from areas of the fabric. So, the tighter you tie, the more defined and clear the resisted area will be. Looser tying will produce more of a dye-bleed effect.

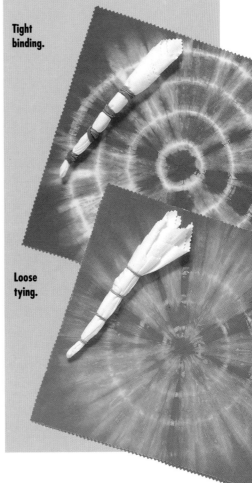

Tight binding.

Loose tying.

12

BINDING MATERIALS

Anything that will fasten around the fabric – string, rubber bands or plastic wrap, can be used as binding. String will give a less defined result since it will absorb some dye during the process, while plastic wrap, will give a clean result it will resist dye completely.

String gives a diffused effect.

Plastic wrap results in a much clearer design.

13 **TWISTING AND FURLING** To create circles and sunbursts, twist or furl the fabric before you tie. Your finished design will depend specifically on how tightly you twist or furl the fabric, how tightly you tie it, and how many ties you place along the twist.

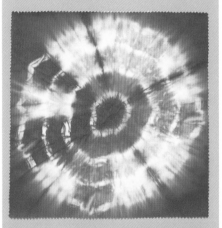

The finished result of twisting and furling.

Bind the fabric tightly after twisting it.

14 **CLUMP TYING** To produce a series of small circles on your fabric, tie one or more solid objects such as corks, rice grains, beans, beads, buttons, pebbles or shells into it either at random or according to a planned design. Harder items may damage the fabric or your washing machine, so you should then use a hand-dye method.

1 legumes
2 rice
3 corks
4 buttons
5 pebbles

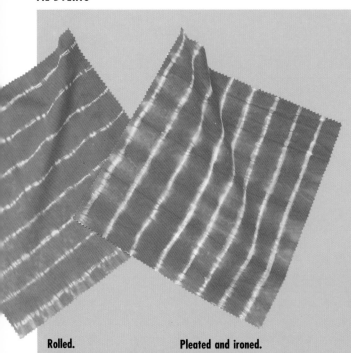

15 **STRIPES** Folding, pleating and rolling the fabric all produce stripes in the finished design, although folding or pleating give a more clearly defined result than rolling. Again, the tightness of the folds affects the crispness of the stripes. Ironing the creases or pleats in the fabric produces very clean, sharp lines. After folding the fabric, secure it at each end.

Rolled.   Pleated and ironed.

16 **CHECKS** To make a checked pattern, follow the technique for stripes, but in two stages. Create the striped pattern first, then after dyeing and ironing, turn the fabric at 90° and fold, roll or pleat along the length, then bind and dye.

After the first dye stage, turn the fabric 90° and dye again.

SCRUNCHING To create a random, marbled effect, scrunch the fabric into a ball and bind it tightly. After the first dye process, this effect can be enhanced by undoing the ball, repeating the scrunching and tying, then putting the new ball through a second color dye process.

The result of two dye processes.

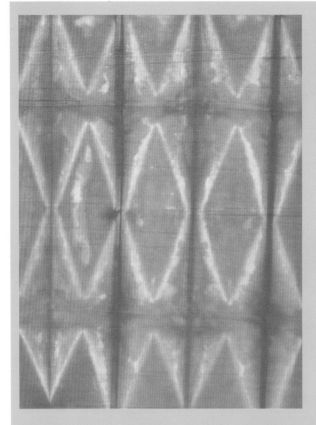

18 **SPRING CLIPS AND CLOTHES-PINS** To give quite a different result from narrow bindings such as string and rubber bands, use heavy spring clips or clothespins. After folding or pleating your fabric, securing it with diagonally placed clips or clothespins will give a chevron pattern across the stripes in the final design.

Chevron pattern using spring clips.

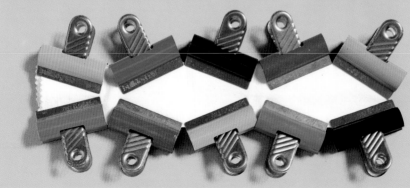

19 **TRITIK** Sewing a running stitch around the edge of a simple hand-drawn design, pulling the thread tight and knotting it will create a delicate, pretty effect in the shape of the original design. Strong thread, such as cobblers' thread, is a must, both to create enough definition to resist the dye, and to stand up to the dyeing process.

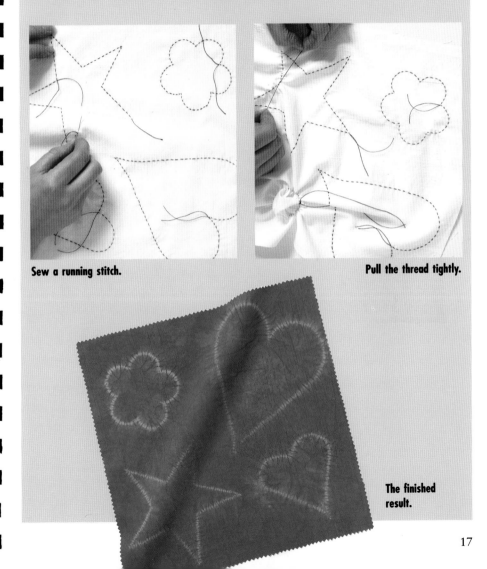

Sew a running stitch.

Pull the thread tightly.

The finished result.

17

20 **DIPPING** You can achieve an unbroken block of color on a specific area of fabric by just dipping the fabric into a dye solution. Use a concentrated solution of a hand dye, dip the chosen area into a bowl containing the solution, leave for 15 minutes, remove, dry and wash to remove any residue.

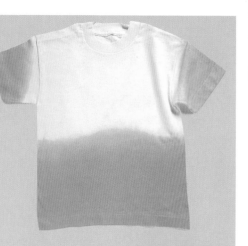

Dipping a T-shirt gives a dramatic effect.

21 **OMBER** This is a wonderful gradated effect, with the color changing from dark to light along the length of the fabric. It is achieved by following the dipping method in 20 and removing the fabric from the dye bath a little at a time at approximately three minute intervals. A 1-yard length of fabric should be removed from the dye bath in about six stages. Results can vary considerably with this technique, but practice and experiment really do make perfect.

Gradually remove the T-shirt from the dye bath for a more subtle effect.

22 **SPIRALING** To create a spiraled effect, put your fabric flat on a surface, pinch the center, twist it into a spiral and secure with two rubber bands to hold the four sections in place. Apply different colors to the sections with a paintbrush or a syringe, using a concentrated dilution of the dye. Seal the finished fabric in a plastic bag and leave it overnight. Usually dyes applied with a brush or syringe will be less colorfast, but using a concentrated dilution and leaving it overnight will make up for this.

Twist the fabric.

Carefully apply concentrated dye solution with a syringe.

A psychedelic spiraling effect.

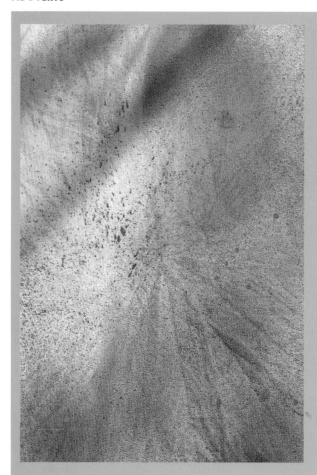

23 **SPRAYING** A plant mister makes a most effective way of applying dye to fabric for specific effects. Dilute a package of dye in a maximum of 2–2½ cups of water and build up delicate tones and shades on the fabric; you can even overlap more than one color. The distance you hold the spray away from the fabric will affect the depth of color. By masking off areas using taped-on stencils, controlled shapes and designs can be created. Leave overnight before rinsing and washing.

24 **MICROWAVES** It is the heat applied to the dye that sets it into the fabric, so a quick and easy method of achieving a tie-dye effect is to place small items in a dye bath using a hand-dye product and put them in a microwave, set on HIGH, for about four minutes. Any metal studs, zippers or catches should be removed before putting a garment in the microwave. This technique should not be used for synthetic and wool-blend fabrics.

FABRIC PAINTING

Though natural fabrics give best results, any fabric can be painted. The color choice of fabric paints is huge and varied, and colors can easily be combined just as with artists' paint. Some fabric paints are translucent and others are opaque, and all can normally be diluted with water. Most fabric paints need to be set with an iron. Always follow the manufacturers' directions on the bottle.

25 **PREPARING YOUR FABRIC** A clear, clean canvas is essential for successful fabric painting, so always wash and iron your fabric before you begin. Place a piece of thick paper, cardboard or styrofoam beneath the fabric or top layer of your garment to prevent the paint from seeping through and use masking tape to secure the fabric to your work surface to prevent slipping.

Slip cardboard inside the T-shirt to protect the back.

26 **TESTING THE COLOR** Fabrics vary in the way they take up paint, and paints, too, can vary from one manufacturer to another, so always try a small amount of paint on a hidden area of the fabric to test the result before you begin.

27

ADEQUATE PAINT If you are combining or diluting color, always mix more paint than you think you need. This will allow you to keep your color even right across the fabric. It is difficult to match shades halfway through a finished piece of work.

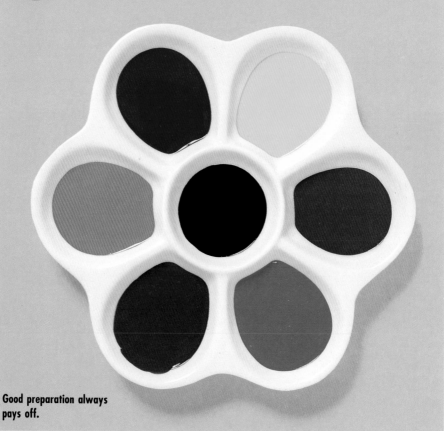

Good preparation always pays off.

28

PAINTING DIRECTION To avoid smudging the paint halfway through your work, always paint from top to bottom and from left to right, or vice versa if you are left-handed.

29 **APPLYING THE DESIGN** If you are painting a freestyle design, apply an outline to the fabric with a fabric marker pen, chalk or a soft pencil. Alternatively, copy your design on a piece of tracing paper with a soft pencil, flip the paper over and go over the outlines on the second side. Then, secure the tracing paper to the fabric with masking tape and rub it onto the fabric.

Use tracing paper to transfer an outline.

This makes painting your design much easier.

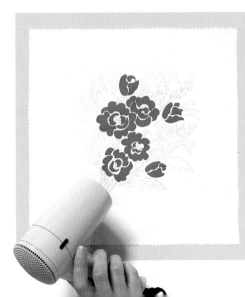

30 **FAST DRYER** It is important to work slowly and methodically and to allow painted areas of your design to dry before adding more color. You can, however, speed up the drying process by using a hairdryer.

23

31 **PAINT DILUTION** Use a more diluted paint to make a wash for larger areas. Wet the fabric first to avoid tidemarks, then use thicker paint for detail in the design.

A wash gives a good background.

Add detail when the wash is dry.

Gradated effects from light to dark.

32 **GRADATED EFFECTS** To create a gradated color effect, work from light to dark, adding a darker color in small amounts to your lighter base color and building up the darker areas.

33 OUTLINING COLORS

To pull your design together, apply a thin line of black paint between areas of color. This will help to define the colors and will give your finished design a lift.

34 DARK INTO LIGHT

If you find that some paint colors will not show up when applied to dark fabrics, making it difficult to work, first paint the design in white. Apply the color when the white undercoat has dried and been set. The colors will then show up more brightly.

Paint over a white undercoat.

35 SPONGING

To add an interesting dappled effect, lightly dab a small natural sponge in the paint, removing any excess by dabbing onto paper towels, and apply to the fabric to achieve an open-textured pattern. This can be further enhanced by overlapping additional colors. It is very important to wash and dry the sponge between each color application. This technique is particularly effective on lampshades where light shines through the design.

Sponging is a simple but effective way of brightening up a room.

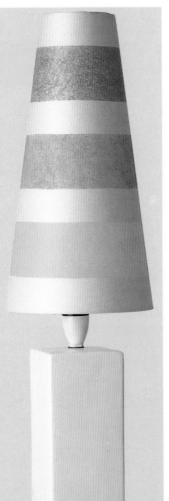

36 SPRAYING

A gentle diffused effect that makes a lovely background can be achieved using a plant spray. Dilute the paint in water before you put it into the spray

A doily makes an attractive stencil.

37 LIFTING

OFF Blot any mistakes with paper towels as soon as possible, then either lightly dab them away with a damp sponge, or camouflage them by painting over with a color that matches the fabric.

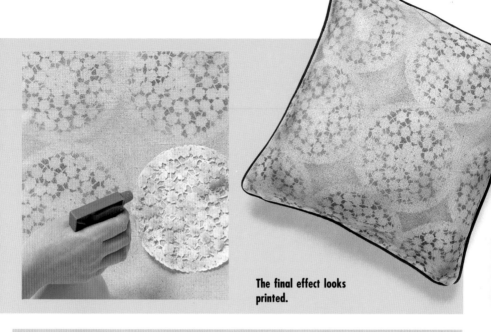

The final effect looks printed.

38 **DRIPPING**
To create a random effect, slightly dilute your paint and carefully drizzle the paint across the fabric with a brush. While it is still wet, use a hairdryer, set on cold, if you can, to blow the paint in different directions.

Drip the paint for a "modern art" effect.

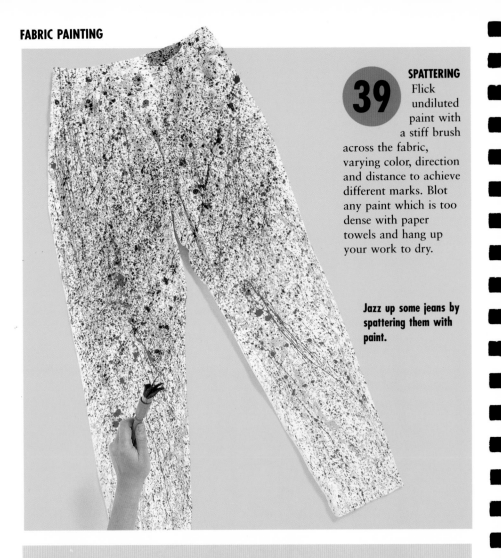

39 SPATTERING
Flick undiluted paint with a stiff brush across the fabric, varying color, direction and distance to achieve different marks. Blot any paint which is too dense with paper towels and hang up your work to dry.

Jazz up some jeans by spattering them with paint.

40 CARE OF STENCILS To prolong the life of your stencils, always wash or wipe them clean after each use. To repair any breaks or tears, fasten with tape on both sides of the stencil, then trim with a craft knife.

41 **STENCILING** Virtually anything that masks off an area of background can be described as a stencil. You can either buy ready-made stencils or cut your own using heavy paper or cardboard and a craft knife. For successful results secure the stencil to the fabric with masking tape and stub the paint through the stencil onto the fabric using a stencil brush with a flat end. Do not overload your brush with paint. As an alternative to a stencil, pieces of masking tape can be used to make shapes on the fabric.

Cut out shapes carefully with a craft knife.

Stub paint over the cutout area.

A great printed effect.

29

42 **DOILYS**
Paper doilys make excellent stencils and are a cheap alternative to those you can buy in craft stores.

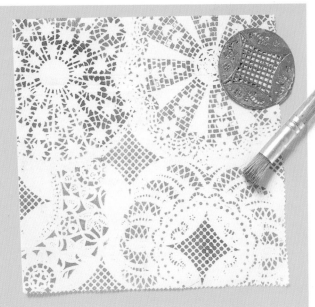

Doilys make excellent and very cheap stencils.

43 **FABRIC PAINTING PENS**
These are widely available and should be used as a marker pen would be on paper. They are very good for outlining and blocking in, but they are not as versatile as paints. You can also use them to achieve an interesting pointilist effect by stabbing at the fabric and building up colors. This technique works best when used with stencils and masked-off areas to give the designs a clearly defined edge.

Pour your paints into wallpaper paste.

44 **MARBLING** Although there are many commercial marbling products on the market, with a little care and practice you can achieve spectacular results with ordinary fabric paints. Using a plastic tray large enough to accommodate your fabric, fill it with wallpaper paste mixed quite thickly. Dribble undiluted paint onto the surface of the paste and drag through with an Afro comb or a fork to make a pattern. Gently lay the fabric on the surface of the paste, then lift it off and rinse the fabric under cold running water to remove the paste. Set the paint according to the manufacturers' directions when the fabric is dry.

Gently swirl them around with a comb.

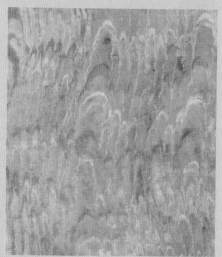

Finished marbled effect.

EMBELLISHING

There is a huge variety of commercial fabric decoration products which can add interesting effects to a painted design. They generally come in bottles with their own applicator and usually have a three-dimensional quality. Glossy, glittery, pearlized, puff, transparent and even fluorescent paints are readily available. Read the manufacturers' directions carefully before you start.

45 **CONTROLLING THE PAINT FLOW** If you have had difficulty with these decoration paints before, it is worth persevering. Most come in bottles or tubes with an applicator nozzle, and they require a little bit of practice before you can use them to their best effect. Try them out on a small piece of scrap fabric first to get the measure of the paint flow. Take care to hold the nozzle slightly above the fabric surface, clearing blocked nozzles with a pin from time to time. It is important not to drag the paint across the fabric, but to apply it smoothly, like frosting a cake.

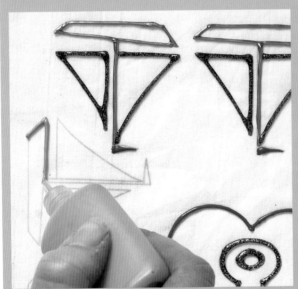

Practice makes perfect with bottled fabric paints.

46
OUTLINING If you have any ragged edges on your painting, then cover them up by outlining with decorative dimensional paint. Areas of fabric paint color can also be given a lift by outlining the shape with these paints.

47
HEAT-EXPANDING PAINTS Read the directions carefully before you use decorative paints. Some of these paints are heat-expanding and need an iron to produce their final result. They invariably spread when dried, so bear this in mind when planning your design. When heat-expanding paints dry, they become quite heavy, so it is best to restrict their use to heavier fabrics.

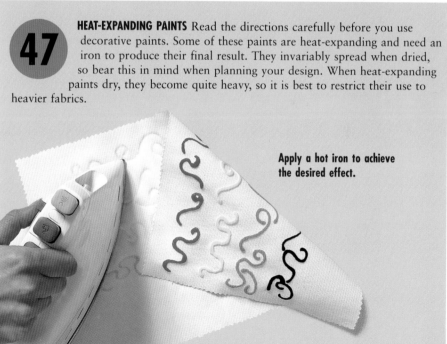

Apply a hot iron to achieve the desired effect.

CARE Most decorative paints do not need heat setting, but the finished garments can be pressed with a cool iron. Iron the garment on the reverse of the fabric, because contact with the paint is bad for the iron as well as the artwork.

 BEADS AND SEQUINS Decorative paints make an excellent adhesive for attaching beads or sequins to a garment. They are particularly effective if the beads are transparent so the color of the paint will show through.

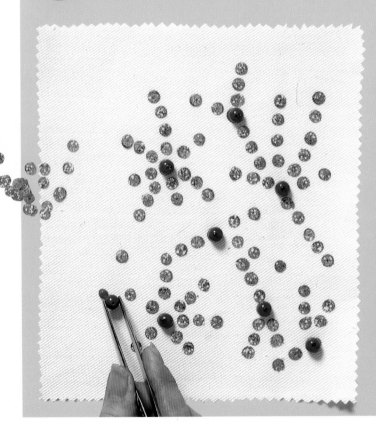

You can use paints to attach sequins and beads.

STITCHING EFFECTS Small crosses of decorative paint applied to fabric really do look like stitched designs.

Create a sampler with paint stitches.

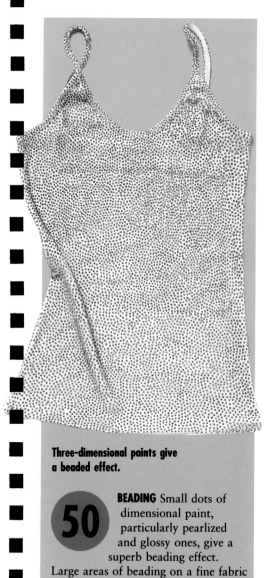

Three-dimensional paints give a beaded effect.

50 **BEADING** Small dots of dimensional paint, particularly pearlized and glossy ones, give a superb beading effect. Large areas of beading on a fine fabric will produce a wonderful result, as if the fabric is heavily beaded.

52 BLOCKING

For an effective way of blocking in areas of a design, use three-dimensional paints. Outline the shape first, leave it to dry and then fill in the center area, working from top to bottom.

Outline your design first.

Fill in once the outline has dried.

53 APPLIQUÉ

Dimensional decorative paint is an excellent outliner for appliquéd fabric designs, and it can hide a multitude of sins. Normally, pieces of appliqué fabric are sewn onto the base fabric; but if you use fusible webbing to attach the fabric pieces, decorative paints used as an outliner can help keep the appliqué anchored.

PRINTING

Printing designs onto fabric using a variety of unusual objects to apply the paint is very simple. Working this way, you can produce very complicated designs, as you can use repeat patterns to create tighter, more controlled designs.

55 **BLOTTING PAPER** To control the density of the paint, make sure you have a supply of blotting pads to remove excess paint from the printing block as you work.

54 **GETTING READY** A slightly padded work surface can make printing much easier, so put a blanket or several layers of fabric under your painting surface. Make sure your fabric is firmly secured to the work surface with masking tape and make sure the work surface or a second layer of fabric is protected by placing heavy paper, cardboard or styrofoam under the top fabric layer.

PRINTING

MATCHING REPEATS If you have ever spoiled a repeat pattern by failing to match the repeats accurately, then make a guide mark on your printing block and measure regular guide marks across and down the fabric. Then match them up as you print to give a regular, even design.

Match repeats by making guide marks along the length of your fabric.

THE PRINTING BLOCK Virtually any solid object can be used as a printing block – from children's building blocks to the ends of crosshead screws. Hard objects will produce more precise, defined prints, whereas a softer item, such as a sponge, will produce less defined, softer images.

Use anything and everything as a printing block.

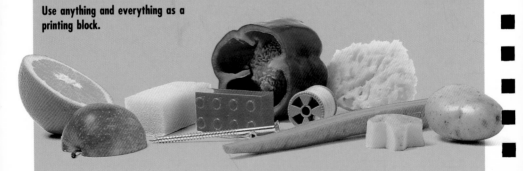

58 **HANDS AND FINGERS** In addition to producing interesting designs, using your hands and fingers to apply paint to fabric is great fun. Apply the paint to your hand with a brush for more precise, defined images, or dip your hand flat into a tray of paint for a denser, less well-defined result. Wash your hands immediately after you finish, since fabric paint has a tendency to stain.

Using your hands can be great fun.

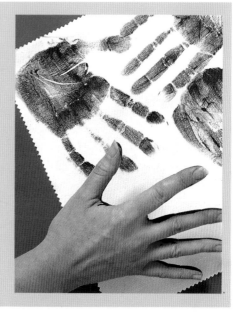

59 **VEGETABLES AND FRUITS** Excellent printing blocks which are always on hand are fruits and vegetables. Either use the natural shapes and texture of, say, a pepper or a mushroom, or cut a design into them – potatoes work best for this. Leave them to dry for 24 hours before you use them. Because they are very absorbent, make sure you have plenty of paper towels handy to blot them before you apply them to the fabric.

Create interesting natural shapes with sliced fruit and vegetables.

60

LEAVES The filigree pattern on the back of a leaf makes an excellent printing block. Either dip the leaf into the paint and place on the fabric or apply the paint with a brush for a more delicate result. When the leaf is applied to the fabric, put a piece of paper over the top and smooth gently with your hand. Coins work well with this method, too.

Leaves with well-defined vein patterns give the best results.

61 **SAFETY FIRST** Linoleum makes the best material for a specific design. Appropriate tools can be bought from most good craft stores. To make cutting easier, warm the linoleum gently before you begin and remember to cut away from yourself to avoid accidents with the sharp cutting tool. To make application easy, glue the linoleum onto a block of wood and let it dry fully. Best results are achieved by applying the paint with a roller, again available from craft stores.

Linoleum-cutting tools are sharp; always cut away from yourself.

62 **STYRO-FOAM** This makes a good, cheap alternative to linoleum and, like linoleum, can be washed gently and re-used. You can use a craft knife or a scalpel to cut the styrofoam.

String and pipecleaners glued to a piece of wood.

63 **STRING, ROPE AND PIPE-CLEANERS** To create an abstract block with an unusual texture, glue thick string or pipe-cleaners, in an interesting shape, onto a block of wood and allow to dry fully. Apply the paint to the string, rope or pipecleaner with a brush and press firmly onto the fabric.

BATIK

This is a centuries-old Indonesian method of decorating fabrics that can easily be achieved in the home with spectacular results. It uses hot wax in a resist technique which masks off areas of the fabric from dye penetration. The wax penetrates the fabric instead of just sitting on the top and prevents the dye from reaching the masked-off areas of the design.

64 **BEFORE YOU START** Batik works best on clean fabric, free of any commercial dressings or finishes. Fine fabrics work better than those with a heavier weave as the wax has less density to penetrate.

65 **TJANTING TOOLS** It's worth investing in a set of tjanting tools if you are going to do much batik. These are the most popular method of applying wax to fabric. They allow a steady flow of molten wax to reach the fabric, making fine and meticulous work possible. They are best for drawing lines and for filling in large areas with a textured pattern. Electrically operated tjanting tools are available and are easy to use.

The flow of wax is regulated by the size of the nozzle.

66 APPLYING THE DESIGN

To avoid leaving permanent marks on the fabric, sketch your design with a washable marker such as a soft pencil, auto-fade pen or fabric marker.

Pencil marks will wash out.

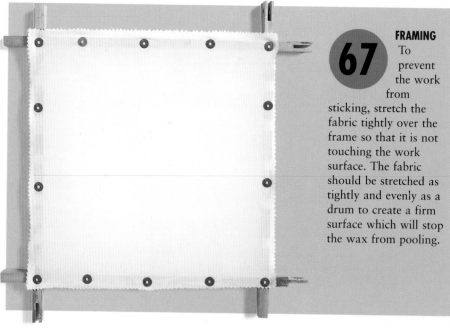

67 FRAMING

To prevent the work from sticking, stretch the fabric tightly over the frame so that it is not touching the work surface. The fabric should be stretched as tightly and evenly as a drum to create a firm surface which will stop the wax from pooling.

68

DRIPS Hold a tissue beneath your tjanting tool or brush as you work to catch any drips. It is essential not to get any spots or drips on the fabric as they will become a part of the design.

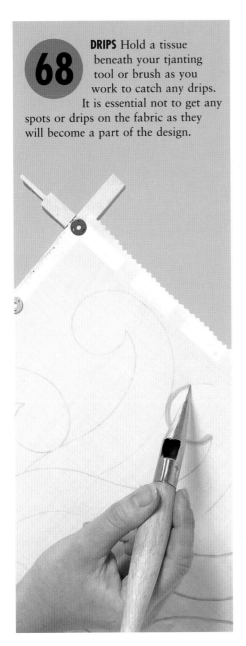

A double boiler works just as well as a professional wax pot.

69

HEATING THE WAX Although there are many good commercial wax pots available, you can just as easily improvise and melt the wax in the top of a double boiler, as if you were melting chocolate. Make sure the wax is heated to the right temperature. Instructions will guide you, but as a general rule of thumb, the wax is at the right temperature when it becomes translucent. Work as fast as you can, as wax cools quickly.

BATIK

70 CHOOSING A WAX

Beeswax or paraffin wax, or a mixture of the two, can be used. Paraffin wax is cheaper, but it becomes more brittle as it dries, giving a slightly different final effect.

71 CRACKLE TECHNIQUE

Paraffin wax is perfect for this technique. The wax literally cracks and allows some dye to seep in, producing a veined effect in the final design; it can look quite spectacular. After the wax has dried, crumple the fabric before you put it through the dye process. Putting the fabric in the refrigerator will make the wax even more brittle and produce a more pronounced effect.

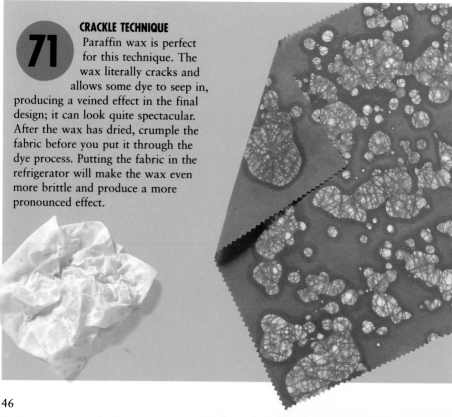

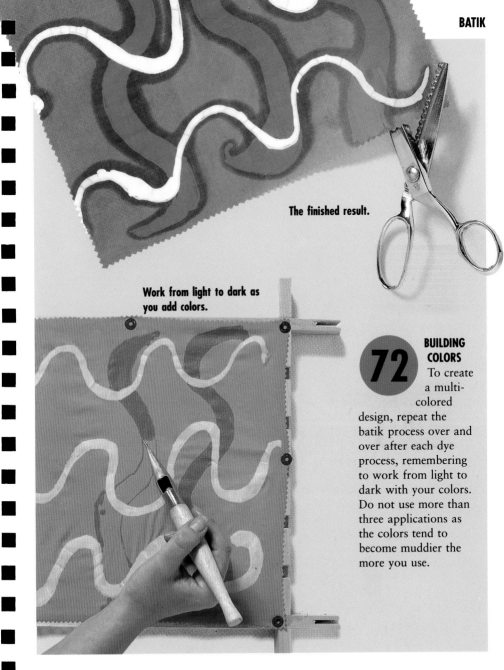

The finished result.

Work from light to dark as you add colors.

72 **BUILDING COLORS**
To create a multi-colored design, repeat the batik process over and over after each dye process, remembering to work from light to dark with your colors. Do not use more than three applications as the colors tend to become muddier the more you use.

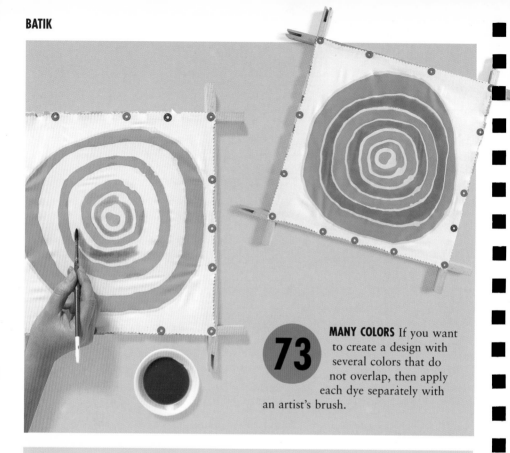

73 **MANY COLORS** If you want to create a design with several colors that do not overlap, then apply each dye separately with an artist's brush.

74 **REMOVING MISTAKES** If you catch a mistake before the wax cools, just blot it away with a paper towel. If the wax has cooled, scrape away as much as you can with a sharp knife, then heat the knife and gently rub it over the area to warm the wax, blotting as you go with a paper towel.

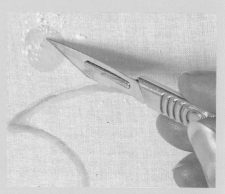

75 **REPEAT PATTERNS** If you want to create a repeat pattern on your design, then use tjaps. These are pieces of metal attached to wooden blocks and are used in the same way as a printing block. Dip the tjap into the hot wax and stamp it onto the fabric to produce your design.

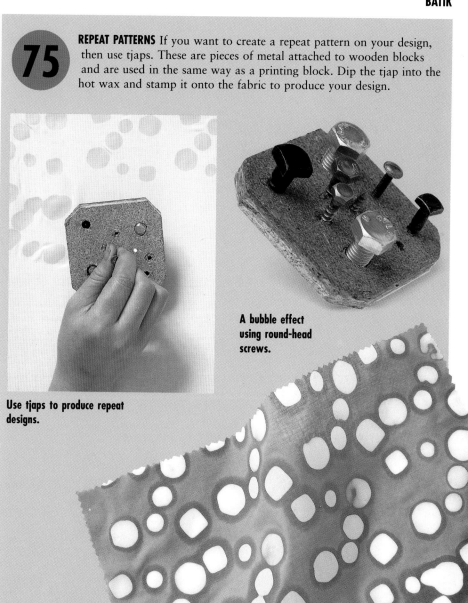

A bubble effect using round-head screws.

Use tjaps to produce repeat designs.

76 **DRIPPING** To create an abstract design very easily, simply drip the wax with a tjanting tool or a brush over the fabric from a height.

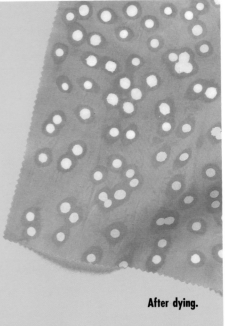

After dying.

Drip the wax.

77 **LINOLEUM BLOCKS** Although linoleum blocks are not generally associated with batik work, they are an excellent way of transferring wax to fabric when you want to incorporate a specific design. Attach a handle to the top of the block so it is easy to dip in the wax.

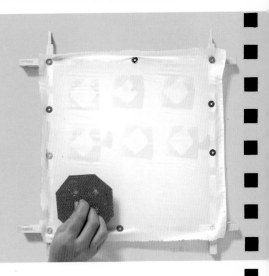

Use linoleum blocks to transfer the wax.

78 **DYE APPLICATION** Only cold-water dyes can be used with batik as hot water will melt the wax. Either put the fabric into a dye bath or apply the dye with a brush. However, if you are using a brush, the dye solution needs to be more concentrated and left overnight to complete its process.

Dye bath.

Painting on a concentrated solution with a brush.

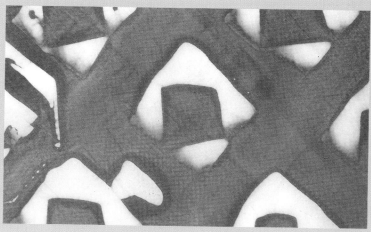

Linoleum blocks are ideal for repeat patterns.

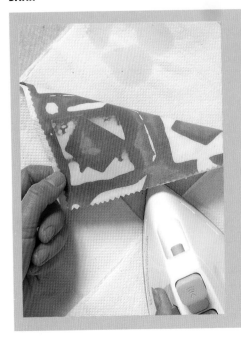

79 **WAX REMOVAL** Once the dyeing process is complete, heat is needed to remove the wax. Normally fabrics are plunged into boiling water, but for delicate fabrics, the best way is to use an iron. Place a piece of paper towel over the fabric and press it with a hot iron, repeating the process until all the wax is removed. A gentle wash in warm water will get rid of any remaining wax.

Use plenty of paper towel when ironing fabric.

80 **DRY CLEANING** Removing wax from delicate fabrics is laborious. There is a commercial dry-cleaning process which works very well, so take delicate fabrics to a good dry cleaner.

81 **BOILING WATER** If you use this method, make sure you do not pour the waxy water down the sink as it will solidify and block the drain. Let the water cool first and skim the wax off the top.

82 **DYE SETTING** Do not be tempted to skip this stage of the dyeing process. It really is crucial. You may have to put your fabric through the wax removal process several times, so it's important that your dye is properly set before you start this part of the process. Even if you put your fabric through a dye-set process, you will lose a little of the color every time you wash it.

SILK PAINTING

Silk fabrics require special paints. These are thin, transparent watercolors which become quite radiant and translucent when applied to silk. Various methods of application lead to many different effects. The nature of the paint necessitates an entirely different technique from many others, but setting is still required.

Different silks produce different results. Test your paint on a small sample.

83 **SILK FABRIC** Before you start to paint, wash and iron your silk to remove any commercial dressings and finishes which may prevent the fabric from absorbing the paint properly. Test a small sample of your silk fabric before you begin to paint as there are many different silks available and each one will react differently to the paint.

84 SKETCHING YOUR DESIGN
To sketch your design onto the silk before you begin to paint, use either a soft pencil or an auto-fade pen, available at most good craft stores.

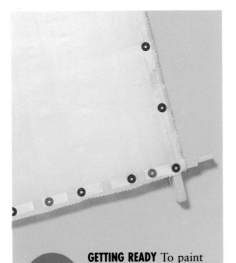

86 DAMP START
To get a wash of color over your silk before you start to paint any specific designs, dampen the silk with a brush or a plant spray. The water will encourage the paint to spread evenly across the fabric. Allow to dry.

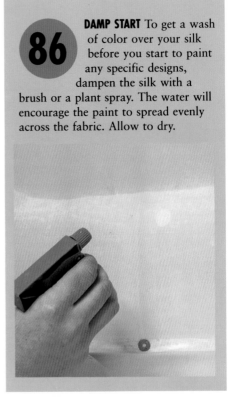

85 GETTING READY
To paint successfully on silk, you need a perfectly even and firm surface. So before you start to paint, stretch your fabric over a frame bound with masking tape to prevent stains. Then, to avoid marking the silk, use three-point architects' pins to attach the silk to the frame.

87

OUTLINERS Silk paints, by their nature, spread over the fabric and need to be controlled. The solution is to create a barrier or resist with a transparent or pigmented gutta to contain the paint within specific areas of the design. Be sure to keep the nozzle of the gutta clean to make sure of even application. Wax can be used as an alternative by following the methods used for batik.

The shimmering colors of silk painting.

Gutta outline.

88 SALT AND SUGAR

Sprinkling coarse salt or sugar onto a wet, painted area, allowing it to dry and then brushing it off will give a marvelous textured effect where the salt has absorbed the color, lightening the immediate area around it. The paint should be damp and not wet, as this will dissolve the salt or sugar. The results are variable and unpredictable, so experiment first.

89 WATERCOLOR TECHNIQUE

To achieve a free-flowing result with silk paints, paint on damp silk as you would with a wash (see 86). Start with small blots of paint, allowing them to spread and grow. Keep the fabric damp as you work to prevent edge-marks from forming.

Work from top to bottom.

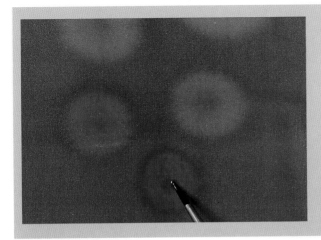

90 **ALCOHOL** Painting alcohol (available from art-supply stores) onto painted areas will dilute the paint to leave paler areas.

91 **OVERLAYING** As with watercolor paints, silk paints can be overlaid to create secondary and tertiary colors. Mask off a design with gutta and paint over it with another color. Remember to work from pale through to dark and to dry the paint between each application. This technique only works with steam-set color and solvent-based gutta.

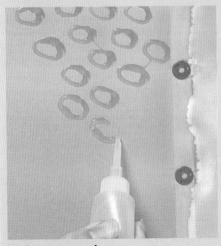

Apply gutta on wash.

Paint a second color on top.

92 **INSTANT DRYING** To prevent a paint application from spreading as much as it would if left to dry naturally, use a hairdryer. Practice the technique of holding the brush in one hand and the hairdryer in the other. This is a particularly useful technique if you are incorporating lots of white areas into your design.

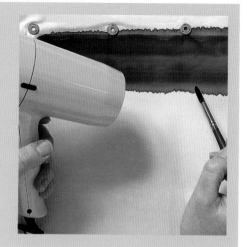

93 **WHITE** Since white paint does not exist, any white in your design must come from unpainted white silk. This means you must plan your design in advance; once paint is applied, it is difficult to remove.

Remember, there is no white silk paint.

TRANSFERS AND READY-MADE DESIGNS

For anybody who does not want to draw freestyle designs, there are many ready-made iron-on transfer kits available. Though the variety is enormous, the technique is simple. You apply the transfer, ink-side down, onto the fabric, secure it with masking tape, and press it with a warm iron. Applying the iron lightly will mean that you can get a couple of repeat prints from each transfer.

94

IMPROVISING Some patterned wrapping papers used by florists and paper bags from stores are made of paper used originally by manufacturers to transfer designs to fabric. Treated as iron-on transfers, they are usually good for one or two more applications, and give best results when used on synthetic fabrics. They are an excellent base for painting or embellishing.

Use a hot iron.

Florists' paper.

Use crayons to make a transfer.

95

MAKING YOUR OWN TRANSFERS If you hanker to create your own transfers, this can be done by drawing designs on paper with inks and crayons specifically made for the purpose. They give you the freedom to experiment and make mistakes before you actually apply your design to the fabric. These designs are applied with an iron in the same way as ready-made transfers.

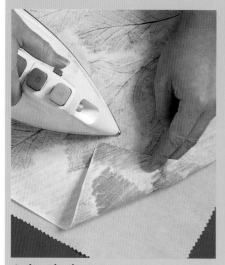

Apply with a hot iron.

IMAGE-TRANSFER PRODUCTS

Recently, a number of products have appeared on the market that allow you to transfer images from paper onto fabric. They can produce quite spectacular results, especially if you add to them with painting or embellishing work.

96

THE IMAGE
The image you use as a transfer must be on a single sheet of paper, so any photographs or book illustrations must be photocopied. Black and white works as well as color. When the image is transferred to the fabric, it will come out in reverse as a mirror image, so if it contains any words or numbers, you should get a reversed photocopy made. Photocopiers can also enlarge or reduce the size of your image, and color laser copies can alter the color of your original image to achieve quite spectacular results.

97 **GETTING PREPARED** To get the best results from this technique, wash your garment or piece of fabric to remove any commercial finishes or dressings, then iron it well so that you have the smoothest canvas possible to work on. If it is a garment, place a piece of cardboard or styrofoam inside to protect the back.

98 **TRANSFER** Brush the transfer medium over the surface of the photocopy, making sure it is evenly and completely covered. Flip the image over and apply it carefully to the fabric, firmly smoothing it down so that the entire image is in contact with the material. Follow the drying instructions on the package, but the longer you can leave it, the better. Overnight is usually the best.

99 **REMOVING THE PAPER** The image is transferred to the fabric by the medium, encapsulating the top layer of the photocopy in a clear plastic coating. To uncover the image, remove the rest of the paper by soaking it well and rubbing with a damp sponge. Remove the last traces by rubbing with your finger.

100 **SETTING AND WASHING** To set the image, apply another layer of the transfer medium to the image and allow it to dry, forming a clear protective coat over the design. Always handwash the finished garment or fabric gently in warm water – it will not usually stand up to machine washing.

CREDITS

The author would like to thank Sarah and Martyn for their help
and support throughout.

Quarto would like to thank the following companies:

Dylon International, Worsley Bridge Rd., Lower Sydenham, London SE26 5HD
for supplying dyes, paints and batik equipment.

George Weil & Sons Ltd, 18 Hanson St., London W1P 7DB for supplying silks
and silk painting products.

Iron-on transfer patterns for tips 33, 51 and 52 used by permission of
Coats Crafts UK.

Art editor Catherine Shearman
Designer Karin Skänberg
Photographers Chas Wilder, Martin Norris
Text editor Anne Crane
Senior editor Sally MacEachern
Editorial director Mark Dartford
Art director Moira Clinch

Typeset by Genesis Typesetting, Rochester
Manufactured in Singapore by Bright Arts (Singapore) Pte Ltd.
Printed in China by Leefung-Asco Printers Ltd.

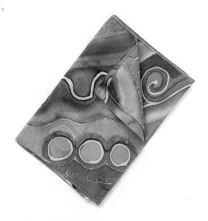